WHEELY GOOD TEAM BUILDING

A Rollerskating Retreat to Revive a Company

SHARON GROSSMAN, PHD

WARRIOR
PUBLISHING

Warrior Publishing, LLC
drsharongrossman.com/contact

ISBN 978-1-952437-02-1

Contents

Contents

CHAPTER 1

The Unlikely Inspiration

A s the final notes of the school play faded, Brian and Brenda clapped enthusiastically for their daughter, Lily, who had just finished her performance alongside her friend, Mia. Lily beamed with pride as she made her way off the stage, her eyes searching for her parents in the crowd.

"There she is!" Brenda exclaimed, pointing towards Lily as she made her way towards her parents.

Lily bounded over, her excitement palpable. "Did you see me, Mom? Dad? Wasn't I great?"

"Absolutely fantastic, sweetheart," Brian replied, ruffling Lily's hair affectionately. "You and your friend were the stars of the show."

As they made their way to the reception area, Brian and Brenda found themselves amidst a flurry of parents congratulating their children on their performances. It was amidst this post-recital buzz that they encountered Tim and Charlotte, Mia's parents.

"Congratulations on a wonderful performance, Lily," Tim said with a warm smile, extending his hand to Brian and Brenda. "And it's lovely to finally meet you both."

"Likewise," Brenda replied, returning the smile. "Lily has been raving about Mia and the play for weeks now."

As the parents exchanged pleasantries, Brian couldn't help but notice the spark of recognition in Tim's eyes.

"I believe Lily mentioned something about you owning a roller skating rink?" Brian asked, curiosity piqued.

Tim chuckled, nodding in affirmation. "That's right. We own the local rink, and my wife, Charlotte, specializes in hosting corporate retreats that use innovative team-building exercises to enhance collaboration and problem-solving skills."

"That sounds fascinating," Brian said. "I run a company myself, a team of 52 people, and we've been struggling with productivity and teamwork lately."

Charlotte, who had joined the conversation, nodded sympathetically. "Those are common challenges in many organizations. Perhaps a change of scenery and some unconventional team-building activities could help."

Brian exchanged a knowing glance with Brenda. Perhaps this chance encounter was exactly what he needed to address the pressing issues plaguing his company. Little did he know, this casual conversation would set the stage for a transformative journey that would challenge his perspectives and redefine his approach to teamwork and productivity.

That night, as Brian and Brenda settled into bed, the conversation with Tim and Charlotte lingered in Brian's mind like a persistent melody. He tossed and turned, the idea of a corporate retreat at the roller skating rink tugging at the edges of his consciousness. Part of him dismissed it as folly, but another part was undeniably riveted by the unconventional approach.

A Daring Decision

Unable to shake the notion, Brian reached for his phone the next morning, his fingers hesitating momentarily before dialing Charlotte's number. She answered on the second ring, her voice warm and familiar despite the early hour.

"Good morning, Brian," Charlotte greeted him, sensing the urgency in his call.

"Morning, Charlotte," Brian replied, his words tumbling out in a rush. "I've been thinking about our conversation last night, and I can't get this idea of a retreat at the roller skating rink out of my head. Can you tell me more about how it works?"

Charlotte chuckled softly, her tone affectionate. "I thought you might be interested. Well, it typically starts with an assessment phase, where we gather information about your company's goals, challenges, and team dynamics. Then we customize the retreat to address those specific needs."

Brian's curiosity grew even stronger. "And what does the retreat itself entail?"

"Usually, it's a three-day program," Charlotte explained. "We incorporate a mix of workshops, team-building activities, and reflective exercises, all centered around the metaphor of roller skating. It's designed to foster collaboration, boost morale, and address any areas of improvement within the team."

Brian nodded thoughtfully, his mind racing with possibilities. "Sounds intriguing. Can you send over a proposal?"

"Of course," Charlotte replied, her voice brimming with enthusiasm. "I'll have it to you within the hour."

A Deeper Look

True to her word, Brian found the proposal in his inbox shortly thereafter. After a quick review and some deliberation, he wasted no time in giving Charlotte the green light to proceed. She, in turn, wasted no time in scheduling an assessment session to dig deeper into the specific needs of Brian's company.

During the assessment, Charlotte observed several key areas where the company could benefit from the roller skating retreat:

1. Some employees displayed resistance to change, clinging to familiar practices and routines. This reluctance to adapt hindered the company's ability to innovate and respond effectively to evolving industry trends.

2. A web of communication challenges – unclear expectations, missed messages, and misinterpretations – tangled the team, leading to conflicts and stalled collaboration. This tense environment choked productivity and morale.

3. The rapid growth of the company led to a lack of cohesion and collaboration among team members. Without a strong sense of unity and shared purpose, employees struggled to work together effectively, leading to inefficiencies and missed opportunities for synergy.

4. Increased workload and stress levels among employees resulted in longer working hours and heightened stress, impacting overall well-being and productivity. Implementing strategies to manage workload and stress is crucial for maintaining employee health and performance.

5. Prioritizing rapid growth, the company hadn't invested in building a strong culture, leaving them vulnerable to issues like high turnover and a disengaged workforce. In fact, without clear guidelines, employees were complaining about a lack of work-life balance.

As Charlotte gathered these insights, she knew that the roller skating retreat held the potential to address these challenges head-on and lead Brian's company toward a path of renewed synergy and success.

CHAPTER 2

The Skating Lesson

❧

The crisp morning air carried with it a sense of anticipation as Brian's team gathered outside the roller skating rink. A mix of excitement and apprehension flickered in their eyes, like popcorn kernels on a hot stove, unsure of whether this unconventional retreat would be a delightful pop or a burnt disappointment. Brian, usually radiating confidence, couldn't quite mask a hint of doubt as his gaze swept across his team.

"Alright everyone, let's head inside," Brian announced, gesturing towards the entrance of the rink.

With hesitant steps, the team followed him into the brightly lit interior of the rink, where the rhythmic beat of music pulsed through the air. The sight of the polished wooden floor stretching out before them, adorned with colorful lights and a disco ball, elicited a mixture of excitement and trepidation from the group.

As they gathered near the center of the rink, Charlotte emerged from the sidelines, her presence commanding attention. With a warm smile, she greeted the team, her eyes alight with enthusiasm.

"Welcome, everyone," Charlotte began, her voice carrying over the hum of conversation. "Today marks the beginning of our journey together—a journey of self-discovery, growth, and transformation."

She paused, allowing her words to sink in before continuing, "But before we dive into the heart of our retreat, I want to start with something simple yet profound: the act of roller skating."

A ripple of uncertainty passed through the group as Charlotte's words hung in the air. Without further ado, she motioned for the team to lace up their roller skates, encouraging them to step onto the rink without any prior instruction.

Individual Challenges

Brian watched as his team tentatively approached the edge of the rink, some with eager anticipation and others with visible hesitation. He felt a surge of anxiety rise within him, unsure of what to expect from this unorthodox approach to team-building.

With a deep breath, Brian joined his team on the rink, feeling the smooth wooden surface beneath his skates as he tentatively glided forward. The sensation was both exhilarating and unsettling, his muscles tense with the effort of maintaining his balance.

Sharon Grossman, Ph.D.

Around him, he could see his team members grappling with similar challenges, their movements awkward and uncertain as they navigated the unfamiliar terrain. Some clung to the edges of the rink for support, while others ventured tentatively into the center, their faces a mixture of determination and fear.

Amidst the chaos of wobbly strides and nervous laughter, Brian noticed distinct personalities emerging within the group.

- **The Perfectionist:** Sarah meticulously adjusted her skates and carefully tested each stride, determined to master the technique flawlessly before venturing further onto the rink.

- **The Daredevil:** Meanwhile, James embraced the challenge with reckless abandon, pushing his speed to the limit as he weaved effortlessly through the crowd.

- **The Hesitant:** Beside them, Emily struggled to find her footing amidst the chaos, her gaze darting anxiously between her colleagues as she sought reassurance and approval.

- **The Observer:** At the opposite end of the rink, Michael hovered near the edges, preferring to observe from a safe distance rather than risk humiliation in the spotlight.

9

Moments of Support and Resilience

As the morning wore on, Brian observed a myriad of reactions unfolding before him: some team members gave up in frustration after a few unsuccessful attempts, while others rallied to support their struggling colleagues with words of encouragement and outstretched hands.

In the midst of it all, Brian couldn't help but notice the presence of one team member who stood out from the rest: Lisa, the blind skater, who moved with a grace and confidence that belied her disability. Guided by Alex, a trusted colleague, she glided effortlessly across the rink, her movements fluid and assured as she navigated the space with ease and confidence.

Throughout the 90-minute session, the team grappled with the challenges of roller skating, each one confronting their fears and insecurities head-on as they sought to master the art of balance and control. Laughter mingled with frustration as they stumbled and fell, only to rise again with renewed determination.

As the session drew to a close, Charlotte motioned for the team to retreat to a private conference room adjacent to the rink, where a healthy lunch awaited them. Exhausted but exhilarated, Brian and his team shuffled off the rink, feeling the soreness in their backs, legs, and hips from the morning's exertions. The physical demands of roller skating had left them ravenous. With eager anticipation, they settled into their seats, ready to refuel their bodies and minds for the challenges the coming three days would bring.

CHAPTER 3

A Glimpse Through the Looking Glass

∽

With lunch finished, Charlotte wasted no time. She addressed the group, her voice carrying a sense of excitement. "Now that we're all refreshed, let's delve into the heart of our retreat. But first, let me introduce you to this room's unique feature."

With a dramatic flourish, Charlotte gestured towards the mirrored wall at the far end of the room. "Behold, the one-way mirror," she announced, a mischievous smile playing on her lips.

Brian and his team exchanged curious glances, their interest piqued by the unexpected revelation.

"What does this mean?" Sarah asked, her brow furrowed in confusion.

Charlotte chuckled, her eyes alight with amusement. "It means that while we can see through this mirror into the roller skating rink, the people on the other side cannot see us. It's an opportunity for us to observe the general public as they skate, without them being aware of our presence."

Becoming Keen Observers

As if on cue, the rink doors swung open, and a flood of skaters entered the arena, their laughter and chatter filling the air. Brian and his team watched in fascination as children and adults of all ages glided across the floor, their movements ranging from clumsy to graceful.

"Before we dive in," Charlotte said, turning her attention back to the group, "I would like a volunteer."

Alex agreed to step up.

"Now, here's your assignment," Charlotte continued. "I want each of you to take five minutes to observe the skaters. Pay attention to their movements, their interactions, and any patterns you notice. Instead of each of you jotting down your observations, I want you to yell out what you see. This way, everyone can participate, and it ensures that Lisa is in the loop. Alex, you capture it all on the whiteboard."

At first, there was a moment of hesitation as the team struggled to find something to comment on. Charlotte sensed their uncertainty and encouraged them to focus on the skaters' attitudes towards skating. "How would you describe their approach?" she prompted.

A Tapestry of Behaviors

James spoke up first. "I see some skaters diving in fearlessly, taking risks with daring spins and jumps," he observed, his eyes scanning the rink. "They're confident, adventurous, like they're fully immersed in the experience."

Sarah, added, "On the other hand, I notice some skaters hesitating at the edges, tentatively testing the waters before venturing further. They seem cautious, perhaps lacking confidence in their abilities."

Emily, an admin assistant known for her empathy, pointed out, "I see skaters helping each other out, offering a hand to those who stumble or cheering on beginners. There's a sense of camaraderie and support, like they're all in it together."

Michael, a deeply introverted bookkeeper, had a penchant for analysis. He noticed that there were also skaters who seemed frustrated or agitated, perhaps struggling with the learning curve or feeling overwhelmed by the crowd. "Their body language suggests tension and stress," he observed.

As the team continued to share their observations, Alex diligently captured their insights on the whiteboard, documenting the diverse behaviors and attitudes observed on the rink. Despite their efforts, the team still seemed puzzled, unsure of how these observations related to their own experiences and challenges in the workplace.

Reflections and Revelations

Sensing their confusion, Charlotte encouraged them to shift gears, still not revealing the point of the exercise. "Now, let's take a moment to reflect on your own skating journey," she suggested. "Share with the group what you encountered, what you felt, and what you learned."

Sarah jumped right in. "I'll admit, stepping onto that rink was nerve-wracking," she confessed, her voice tinged with uncertainty. "If I'm honest, I was scared I'd fall and make a fool of myself in front of you all. I was so in my head, worrying about every move I made, that I didn't much enjoy the experience. Looking back, I realize I missed out on the fun because I was too focused on avoiding mistakes."

Michael nodded in agreement, adding, "I found myself out of my comfort zone, stumbling and struggling to find my balance. It was frustrating at times, but also incredibly rewarding when I finally managed to glide across the floor."

During the lull, Alex shared, "I was guiding Lisa. So, we were skating together, holding hands, and I had to think ahead as we approached the turns to make sure I signaled to her on time. I felt a strong sense of responsibility to ensure she was safe, but once we got the hang of it, I was able to enjoy myself and take pride in the knowledge that Lisa was also enjoying herself. Seeing her courage and resilience inspired me to push through my own doubts."

This was the perfect moment for Lisa to talk about the experience from her perspective. Without prompting, she said, "As someone who is visually impaired, skating was a whole new world for me. It was scary at first, relying on Alex to guide me, but as I gained confidence, I felt a sense of freedom and empowerment. And I'm so grateful for you, Alex. You did a great job!"

Brian, the CEO, cleared his throat, preparing to share his own skating experience. "I have to admit, it was quite the adventure," he began with a chuckle. "It's been years since I last put on a pair of roller skates, and let's just say, it wasn't like riding a bike. At first, it was all fun and games, but after about 60 minutes, I found myself glancing at the clock, wondering how much longer I had to endure."

Finally, one of the managers, Sheila, raised her hand, eager to share her own insights. "For me, watching the team on the rink was eye-opening," she began, her tone thoughtful. "I noticed how some of us were hesitant and unsure, much like Sarah described. But there were others who seemed to take to it effortlessly, gliding around with confidence and grace."

Charlotte smiled warmly at the team, impressed by their engagement and willingness to share their experiences. "You all did a fantastic job both in your observations and in expressing your own experiences," she praised. "I know you're curious about how all of this ties into our retreat objectives, and I promise that will become clear by the end of our time together."

CHAPTER 4

Brainstorming Solutions

∾

After a short break, Charlotte divided the team into five groups, each consisting of 10-11 individuals. "Now, let's leverage the insights we've gained so far and dive deeper into addressing our key themes," she explained. "Each group will have a chance to brainstorm ideas related to one of the following themes: communication, change management, collaboration, workload management, and work-life balance."

Charlotte pointed to the five whiteboards on the wall, each labeled with a theme. "We'll have a rotating brainstorming session. Each group will spend 10 minutes discussing their assigned theme and jot down ideas on the corresponding whiteboard. After the timer goes off, you'll rotate clockwise to the next theme, adding your contributions to a new board."

With a nod from Charlotte, the teams dispersed, each huddling around their designated whiteboard, markers poised and minds brimming with ideas.

Crystallizing Ideas

At the 50-minute mark, Charlotte called out. "Alright everyone, let's regroup! Each group, please identify the most promising idea for your theme and circle it for easy reference."

The teams huddled again, debating the merits of their ideas before circling their top pick. Anticipation hung in the air as everyone awaited the presentations.

"Let's start with communication," Charlotte said. Ashley, the self-proclaimed team cheerleader, stepped forward.

"Our group came up with 'Coffee Chats,' short, informal gatherings over coffee or tea. Anyone can sign up to host a chat, inviting colleagues from different departments to discuss a project, share ideas, or simply get to know each other better. It's a low-pressure way to break down silos and spark conversation."

Charlotte nodded. "Coffee Chats are a great way to build connections across departments in a smaller company setting like yours."

Next, Sheila, a veteran of the company, took the floor. "The 'Change Champions' idea resonated with us. We believe a smaller group of colleagues trained in change management can act as liaisons between leadership and the team, explaining upcoming changes and answering questions. Given our size, we could likely identify 3-4 volunteers who could champion these efforts."

"Absolutely," agreed Charlotte. "A dedicated Change Champion team can ensure smooth transitions and address any concerns early on."

Michael, brimming with enthusiasm, presented the Collaboration team's idea. "We propose a 'SkillSwap' series. Every other week, a colleague from a different department volunteers to share their expertise during a lunchtime session. It's a win-win: the presenter gets to showcase their skills, and the audience learns something new."

Charlotte smiled. "A 'SkillSwap' series is a fantastic way to leverage the diverse skillset you have within a company of your size. It fosters collaboration and knowledge sharing in a fun and engaging way."

James, the team's efficiency champion, presented their workload management proposal. "We came up with 'Focus Fridays,' dedicated days with minimized distractions to tackle deep work tasks," he explained. "Employees wouldn't be scheduled for meetings or interruptions on Fridays, allowing them to focus on their most important priorities."

"This initiative aims to improve individual productivity and reduce workload strain," James continued. "By carving out dedicated focus time, we can ensure employees have uninterrupted stretches to complete complex tasks without feeling overwhelmed."

Charlotte's eyes lit up. "Focus Fridays sound like a strategic way to combat workload challenges. We can track their impact on project completion rates and employee well-being before potentially expanding the program."

Finally, Emily, the team's resident optimist, presented the work-life balance team's suggestion. "We propose creating a 'Wellness Corner' in the office. It would be a dedicated space with comfortable seating, calming music, and resources on healthy living. Employees can utilize this space during breaks to relax, de-stress, or practice mindfulness techniques."

"A Wellness Corner is a thoughtful idea," acknowledged Charlotte. "It shows your commitment to employee well-being and can help reduce stress levels in a cost-effective way for a company of your size."

Moving Forward

Brian, who had been silently observing the presentations, addressed the team. "This has been a fantastic session! Every idea presented shows creativity and a real desire to improve our work environment. We'll take all your suggestions into serious consideration and develop a plan that incorporates the best aspects of each proposal."

As they wrapped up the exercise, Charlotte took a moment to summarize the day's activities and key takeaways.

Looking Back and Looking Ahead

"Thank you, Brian, and everyone for your input. Today has been incredibly productive," Charlotte began, addressing the team with a warm smile. "We've covered a lot of ground and generated some fantastic ideas for addressing your workplace challenges."

She paused, allowing the team to reflect on their accomplishments.

"I, too, am proud of each and every one of you for your creativity, collaboration, and commitment to driving positive change within your organization," Charlotte continued. "But our work doesn't stop here."

Charlotte looked around the room, meeting each team member's gaze. "Tomorrow, we'll continue our journey towards greater teamwork, communication, and productivity. But for now, I want you all to rest and recharge. We have a big day ahead of us."

With that, she dismissed the team, sending them home with a renewed sense of purpose. As they filed out of the conference room, Brian and his colleagues felt energized and optimistic about the progress they had made on day one of the retreat. They knew that with Charlotte's guidance and their collective efforts, they could overcome any challenges that lay ahead.

CHAPTER 5

Communication and Conflict Resolution

≈

The morning sunlight streamed through the windows of the skating rink, bathing the smooth surface in a warm glow. Tim, the instructor, had transformed the space into a playful challenge zone. A series of obstacles – cones, speed bumps, and slalom poles – snaked across the rink, demanding teamwork and coordination to navigate. Divided into teams, the team members gathered at the starting line, a mix of excitement and nervous laughter bubbling in the air.

The Importance of Clear Communication

"Alright, team!" boomed Sarah, her voice brimming with confidence. "Let's conquer those cones first, single file, smooth zigzags!"

With a silent nod of agreement, they launched into action. Sarah weaved through the cones with practiced ease, her teammates mirroring her movements with focused determination. A chorus of encouragement and "watch out for the red one!" filled the air, a symphony of teamwork.

Lisa, partnered with Michael for guidance, leaned in close to him. "Hey, Michael, I trust you to lead me through this. Just keep talking to me, and we'll get through it together," she said, her tone filled with unwavering resolve.

Michael, feeling the weight of responsibility, nodded reassuringly. "You got it, Lisa. Just stay close, and we'll take it one obstacle at a time," he replied, his voice steady despite the adrenaline coursing through him.

James and Emily, working in tandem, maneuvered through the cones with precision, their movements synchronized as they followed Sarah's lead. They communicated seamlessly, offering support and guidance whenever needed.

Across the rink, a different dynamic unfolded. Team Red's expressions were steely, but a flicker of unease danced in their eyes. Their initial attempt at the course revealed their disjointedness. Team members veered off course, frustration mounting as they collided with each other.

Undeterred, Team Blue continued with practiced ease. Even Lisa, her trust in Michael unwavering, navigated the course with surprising grace. Her clear communication and reliance on her partner propelled them forward.

As the course escalated in difficulty, Team Blue's cohesion truly shone. They anticipated each other's moves, seamlessly adjusting their strides to maintain balance and support. Their trust in each other was evident, a stark contrast to Team Red's growing frustration.

In a display of teamwork and synchronized movement, Team Blue crossed the finish line first, erupting in joyous cheers. Team Red watched on, a mix of disappointment and a hint of admiration coloring their faces.

Charlotte and Tim exchanged a knowing glance. The obstacle course had laid bare the communication and trust gap between the two teams. Team Blue's collaborative spirit and clear communication propelled them to victory, while Team Red's disjointed approach hindered their progress.

Debriefing: Building Bridges Through Communication

After the exhilarating race and a well deserved refreshment break, Charlotte gathered the teams in the conference room for a debrief session.

"Wow, that was quite the experience out there," Charlotte remarked, casting a knowing smile around the room. "Let's take a moment to reflect on what we just witnessed."

This time, Tim joined in, standing by the whiteboard, ready to capture their thoughts. "Tim, what did you observe out there?" asked Charlotte.

A thoughtful expression on his face, Tim shared, "Well, it was fascinating to see how differently the two teams approached the obstacles. Team Blue seemed to move as one cohesive unit, supporting and guiding each other through the course. Their communication, or lack thereof, was evident in their expressions and actions."

Charlotte added, "Team Blue's nonverbal cues, like anticipating each other's moves, were crucial for smooth coordination." This sparked a discussion on the importance of non-verbal communication in the workplace.

The Power of Collaboration and Trust

Michael, reflecting on his experience guiding Lisa, shared his perspective. "Even in challenging situations, like guiding Lisa through the obstacles, communication is essential," he noted. "Because I was holding Lisa's hand, I could signal nonverbally through wrist motions which way to go. But ultimately, we needed to trust each other to get through it in one piece."

Lisa, sitting alongside Michael, raised her hand to contribute to the discussion. "I want to share my perspective," she began, her voice steady and resolute. "For me, this race wasn't just about teamwork and communication. It was also about accessibility.

Without Michael's guidance and the support of my teammates, I wouldn't have been able to participate fully. It's a reminder that inclusivity and accommodation are crucial aspects of teamwork and collaboration. By acknowledging and addressing the needs of all team members, we can truly work together towards our shared goals."

"Great reminder, Lisa. Thank you for bringing this to our attention and we are so pleased you had Michael to assist," said Charlotte. "Now," she began, her gaze sweeping across the room, "what about Team Red?"

Identifying Communication Breakdowns

Tim pointed out, "Team Red seemed to struggle and from what I observed, the culprit was a lack of communication which led to confusion and frustration. Does this remind anyone of how you feel at work?" This served as a springboard to discuss conflict resolution.

Tim's question hung in the air, causing a ripple of recognition through the room. Shoulders slumped, and knowing glances were exchanged.

Sarah, the ever-optimistic leader of Team Blue, was the first to break the silence. "Actually, Tim, that does hit a little close to home," she admitted. "There have been times on projects where communication breaks down, and it leads to exactly what you saw with Team Red – confusion and frustration."

James chimed in. "Absolutely, Sarah. Think about the recent marketing campaign. If we had just had clearer communication about deadlines and expectations from the start, a lot of the last-minute scrambling and finger-pointing could have been avoided."

A chorus of agreement rose from the group. Several team members recounted specific instances where communication breakdowns had led to conflict and hindered their work.

Bridging the Gap Between Activity and Reality

Charlotte, seizing the opportunity to bridge the gap between the exercise and their daily challenges, took center stage. "These are all great examples," she acknowledged. "It seems clear that ineffective communication is a significant barrier to your success as a team. But the good news is, just like Team Blue demonstrated on the rink, we can learn to communicate more effectively and navigate these challenges."

Charlotte then turned to the ideas generated during the brainstorming session. "Remember yesterday, when we discussed the concept of 'Coffee Chats'?" she asked, pointing to the whiteboard. "Can anyone see how these informal gatherings could foster better communication across departments and help us avoid misunderstandings in the future?"

Ashley jumped at the opportunity. "Absolutely, Charlotte! Coffee Chats would be a low-pressure way for colleagues to connect, share ideas, and simply get to know each other better. That kind of familiarity often leads to more open and honest communication down the line."

The discussion continued, with team members brainstorming how each proposed solution – from "Change Champions" to "Lunch & Learn" sessions – could contribute to a more communication-focused and collaborative work environment.

Lessons Learned: From Rink to Real World

Charlotte nodded in approval before addressing the team. "Now, take a moment to reflect on your experiences skating yesterday," she said, "and how they connect to the lessons we've discussed."

A thoughtful silence descended as the team members pondered the connection. Sarah, ever the leader, was the first to break the ice.

"On the rink," she began, "clear communication and coordination were key to navigating the obstacles. It's no different at work! Just like on the rink, effective communication and teamwork are essential for our projects and tasks."

James chimed in, building on her point. "Absolutely! And remember non-verbal communication? Team Blue used hand signals and body language – a simple nod or gesture can be powerful in the workplace too!"

Emily nodded in agreement. "And Team Red? Their struggles were a stark reminder of the consequences of poor communication – confusion, frustration, and setbacks. We all need to learn from that."

Michael, reflecting on his experience, added, "Lisa and I learned firsthand how trust and collaboration are reinforced through effective communication. By communicating openly and trusting each other's guidance, we were able to overcome challenges together. It really showed us the value of building strong relationships within our teams."

Charlotte smiled, impressed by their insights. "Well said, everyone. It's clear that your experiences on the rink have provided us with valuable lessons that we can apply to your work. Now, let's think about how this experience relates to our theme of communication and conflict resolution at work."

She pivoted the conversation towards their brainstorming session. "Remember the 'Coffee Chats' idea?" she asked, pointing to the whiteboard.

Brian readily connected the dots between the activities. "On the rink, clear communication helped us succeed. Similarly, Coffee Chats can foster communication across departments, preventing misunderstandings in the future."

Ashley, enthusiastic as ever, built on Brian's idea. "Exactly! Coffee Chats provide a casual space to connect, share ideas, and build relationships. That familiarity can lead to more open communication down the line."

CHAPTER 6

Adaptability: Your Secret Weapon in a Changing Workplace

≫

After a brief break, Charlotte reconvened the team in the conference room.

"Alright, everyone, let's explore our experiences and observations from our activities yesterday and see how they relate to embracing change and adaptability," Charlotte began, standing by the whiteboard, ready to capture their thoughts and insights.

"Yesterday, as we observed the skaters, we saw a wide range of responses to change," Alex began. "Some embraced it wholeheartedly, eagerly trying out new moves and techniques. They adapted quickly to the shifting dynamics of the rink."

Sarah jumped in, as if to finish Alex's thought.. "Yes, and there were others who seemed hesitant to step out of their comfort zone, clinging to familiar routines and resisting change."

"I noticed that some skaters were encouraging and supportive of others who were trying new things," Emily said. "Their willingness to embrace change and help others adapt created a positive and empowering atmosphere on the rink."

"On the flip side, there were also skaters who struggled with change," Michael noted. "They seemed overwhelmed by the unfamiliarity of it all, hesitant to venture beyond their usual routines."

Adaptability in Action: Real-World Parallels

As the discussion unfolded, the team began to reflect on their own experiences navigating the obstacles and challenges on the rink.

"I remember when we encountered that sharp turn on the rink," James recalled, his brow furrowing with concentration. "At first, I was hesitant to adjust my technique, but then I realized I needed to lean into the turn more to maintain my balance."

Sarah nodded in agreement, adding, "I had a similar experience when we came across a slick patch. Instead of panicking, I had to adapt my skating style, taking shorter strides and shifting my weight to avoid slipping."

Emily chimed in, sharing her own encounter with a crowded section of the rink. "When I found myself surrounded by other skaters, I had to adapt quickly, weaving in and out of the crowd while maintaining my balance. It taught me the importance of staying agile and responsive in unpredictable situations."

Michael nodded thoughtfully, recalling a moment when he had to navigate around a fallen skater. "I had to adjust my trajectory at the last minute to avoid a collision," he explained. "It reminded me that change can come unexpectedly, and we need to be ready to adapt at a moment's notice."

Putting It Into Practice: Adaptability in the Workplace

Charlotte listened intently to their stories, recognizing the parallels between their experiences on the rink and the challenges they face in the workplace.

"The lesson here is clear," she remarked, turning to the team. "You all had to adapt your skating techniques to overcome obstacles on the rink. In a similar way, you must be willing to adapt and evolve in the face of change in the workplace. Embracing change and cultivating adaptability is not just a skill—it's a mindset that empowers us to thrive in any situation."

With that, Charlotte encouraged the team to reflect on how they can apply this lesson to their daily work routines. "Think about a recent change or challenge you faced at work," she suggested. "How did you respond to it? What could you have done differently to embrace it more effectively?"

As the team members pondered these questions, Charlotte reminded them of the importance of being proactive in seeking opportunities for growth and learning, even in the midst of change. "Remember," she concluded, "adaptability isn't just about reacting to change—it's about seizing the opportunities it presents and using them to propel yourself and your team forward."

CHAPTER 7

The Power of "We": Collaboration for Success

∼∼

It was time to switch gears. With the insights from their discussion on adaptability still fresh in their minds, Charlotte smoothly transitioned the team's focus to the next topic.

"Alright, team, let's see how our observations from yesterday's activities relate to fostering cohesion and collaboration," Charlotte began, her tone inviting open discussion and reflection.

James was the first to speak up, recalling their observations from the skating rink. "Yesterday, we saw skaters working together, helping each other out when someone stumbled or providing words of encouragement," he noted. "Their willingness to support each other created a sense of cohesion and teamwork."

Sarah nodded in agreement, adding, "It was inspiring to see how teamwork and collaboration were essential for some skaters to perform more complex maneuvers or routines. They relied on each other's strengths and coordinated their efforts to achieve a common goal."

Emily chimed in next, her voice filled with enthusiasm. "I also noticed how skaters who communicated effectively with each other were able to anticipate each other's moves and respond accordingly," she observed. "Their synergy and coordination made them more effective as a team."

The Importance of Communication and Collaboration

Michael, reflecting on their observations, added, "But there were also instances where skaters seemed to struggle with coordination and collaboration. Without clear communication and mutual support, they faced difficulties in working together towards a shared objective."

Charlotte nodded thoughtfully, acknowledging Michael's observation. "You're absolutely right, Michael. Effective communication is the foundation of fostering cohesion and collaboration within a team," she affirmed. "Without it, teams can struggle to coordinate their efforts and may encounter obstacles that could have been easily overcome with proper communication."

Building Relationships and Leveraging Strengths

She then skillfully connected the concept of collaboration to a previously discussed initiative. "Speaking of collaboration, let's consider the SkillSwap Initiative as an example," Charlotte continued. "This program aims to promote cross-departmental collaboration by facilitating knowledge exchange and sharing best practices among employees."

"We must recognize the importance of fostering cohesion and collaboration within our teams," Charlotte emphasized, her voice carrying conviction. "It's not just about completing tasks efficiently; it's about building strong relationships, leveraging each other's strengths, and working towards a shared vision as a unified team."

Emily, visibly moved by the message, nodded in agreement. "Absolutely. When we work together seamlessly, drawing on each other's skills and knowledge, we're able to accomplish far more than when we're each working in isolation."

CHAPTER 8

Beyond the Finish Line: Prioritizing Well-Being for Peak Performance

⚮

As the team transitioned to the topic of addressing workload, Charlotte encouraged everyone to reflect on their observations from the skating rink and how they related to managing stress and workload in the workplace.

"Yesterday, as we observed the skaters," Sarah began, "we noticed how some of them took regular breaks to rest and hydrate, which seemed to help them maintain their stamina and focus."

Emily added, "Yes, and we also saw skaters who appeared to be more relaxed and composed than others. They seemed to have a calm demeanor and were able to recover quickly when the unexpected happened, like when other skaters cut across the rink in front of them."

Charlotte nodded in agreement. "Indeed, taking breaks and maintaining a calm demeanor are important aspects of self-care and mindfulness. It's essential to recognize the value of rest and relaxation in managing stress and workload, both on the rink and in the workplace."

Pacing Yourself and Avoiding Burnout

James spoke up, recalling their own experiences on the rink. "I found that when I focused too much on pushing myself to go faster or perform better, I ended up feeling more stressed and fatigued," he admitted. "But when I paced myself and took breaks when needed, I was able to maintain my energy and focus for longer periods of time."

"That's a valuable insight, James," Charlotte remarked. "It's essential to recognize our limits and practice self-compassion. We wouldn't expect a skater to skate non-stop without rest. Why should we expect ourselves or our team members to work without breaks or downtime?"

The Power of Support and Camaraderie

Michael shared his thoughts, "I also noticed that skaters who supported each other and offered encouragement were better able to manage stress and workload. Their camaraderie created a supportive environment where everyone felt valued and motivated."

Charlotte nodded thoughtfully. "Indeed, social support plays a crucial role in coping with stress. As a team, we need to foster a culture of support and understanding, where team members feel comfortable reaching out for help when needed. Now let's take a moment to reflect on how we can implement these valuable lessons in your workplace to promote well-being and productivity."

"But what if our team members don't feel comfortable seeking help or offering support?" asked Lisa.

Charlotte nodded, "Building a supportive environment takes time and effort," she acknowledged. "As team leaders, it's our responsibility to create opportunities for open communication, collaboration, and team-building activities. Fostering trust and camaraderie encourages a culture where everyone feels valued and supported."

Taking Breaks and Believing You're Worth It

Before anyone had a chance to say much, James raised an objection. "I understand the importance of rest and relaxation, but in our fast-paced work environment, taking breaks might not always be feasible," he noted.

Charlotte nodded, acknowledging James's point. "That's a valid concern, James," she replied. "While it's true that your work demands can be intense, it's essential to recognize that taking short breaks, even just a few minutes, can actually improve productivity and focus in the long run. It's about finding a balance that works for each of us."

Emily chimed in, addressing the need for self-compassion and mindfulness. "But what if we feel guilty or judged for taking breaks or prioritizing our well-being?" she wondered aloud, sharing a common worry among the team.

Setting Boundaries and Advocating for Yourself

Sarah offered her perspective, her tone reassuring. "I understand where you're coming from, Emily. But, prioritizing self-care isn't selfish—it's essential for maintaining our health and performance. We need to set an example and encourage open conversations about well-being so we can help shift the culture to one that values self-care and mindfulness."

Michael raised another concern about pacing oneself and setting boundaries. "But what if our workload is simply too overwhelming to pace ourselves effectively?" he questioned, expressing a common challenge faced in their line of work.

Charlotte listened attentively before responding. "I hear your concern, Michael. In situations where the workload feels overwhelming, it's crucial to communicate with your team and managers about your capacity and priorities. It's important to set clear boundaries and advocate for yourself to prevent burnout. In other words, it's not about how much you can get done, it's about how much you can get done in a sustainable fashion."

Revisiting the "Focus Fridays" Initiative

In response to these concerns, Charlotte suggested revisiting the 'Focus Fridays' idea program proposed during the brainstorming session. She explained, "Remember the idea of dedicating Fridays to focused individual work with minimal interruptions? This program could be a practical way to implement the concept of pacing and setting boundaries. By having a designated day with fewer meetings or distractions, we can create dedicated time for uninterrupted work, potentially boosting productivity and reducing stress levels throughout the week."

The team members seemed receptive to the idea. Ashley, always enthusiastic about new initiatives, chimed in, "Focus Fridays sound great! It would allow us to tackle those deep-focus tasks that often get pushed aside in the daily hustle and bustle."

James, initially skeptical about breaks, seemed intrigued by the potential benefits. "Maybe having dedicated focus time on Fridays would actually free us up to be more productive during the rest of the week, knowing we have that uninterrupted time coming."

The discussion continued, with the team exploring ways to refine and implement the Focus Fridays program. They considered setting clear expectations for communication and availability on Fridays, as well as potential solutions for urgent matters that might arise during those dedicated work periods.

A Well-Deserved Break

With a sense of accomplishment, the team wrapped up their discussion on workload and stress management, feeling optimistic about the potential solutions they had identified. "We've covered a lot of ground so far today," Charlotte remarked, smiling at the team. "Now, I think it's time for a well-deserved lunch break. We can reconvene afterwards to continue our discussions."

The team members readily agreed, eager for a chance to recharge and reflect on the valuable lessons learned throughout the day.

CHAPTER 9

The Importance of Balance

After returning from lunch, the team reconvened with renewed energy to dive into the topic of balance. Charlotte opened the discussion, laying the groundwork for their exploration.

"Before our lunch break, we had some insightful discussions about managing workload and setting boundaries," she began. "Now, let's shift our focus to the broader concept of balance. As skaters, we need to maintain balance on the rink to glide smoothly.

Similarly, we also need to find balance in your work and personal lives to thrive."

James nodded in agreement, recalling his experiences on the rink. "Balancing on skates requires constant adjustments and awareness of our body's movements," he remarked. "Similarly, finding balance in our work requires us to continuously assess our priorities and make necessary adjustments."

Sarah chimed in, sharing her perspective on work-life balance. "I've found that setting clear boundaries between work and personal time is essential for maintaining balance," she said. "Carving out dedicated time for relaxation and hobbies outside of work can recharge our batteries and help us come back to work refreshed and focused."

Emily nodded in agreement, adding, "It's also important to be realistic about our capabilities and commitments. You know, when we're out there skating, we can't perform every trick flawlessly. The same is true at work. We can't excel in every aspect of our work without sacrificing our well-being. We need to prioritize tasks and allocate our resources wisely to maintain balance."

"So true," said Michael. Then, he added, "In skating, we have to distribute our weight evenly to stay balanced. Similarly, in our work, we need to allocate our time, energy, and resources effectively to avoid burnout and maintain equilibrium." Here, Charlotte interjected, building upon Michael's point.

"Absolutely, Michael," Charlotte acknowledged. "And that's where the Wellness Corner, an initiative you all brainstormed yesterday, comes in. Remember, we discussed creating a dedicated space to support a healthy work-life balance."

Charlotte continued, summarizing their discussion and highlighting the key takeaways. "It's clear that finding balance requires intentional effort and self-awareness," she remarked. "We all need to prioritize self-care, set boundaries, and allocate resources wisely. By acknowledging our limitations and actively managing our workloads, we can create a sustainable and fulfilling work-life balance. Remember, the Wellness Corner is here to support us on this journey."

CHAPTER 10

Confidence on Wheels

∼≈∽

Charlotte steered the conversation toward a new topic, one that resonated deeply with their recent skating experiences. "Let's talk about confidence," she began, a glint in her eye. "Remember that exhilarating feeling of finally landing that challenging jump or gliding effortlessly around the rink? Confidence is crucial on skates, but its impact transcends the rink walls. It's a skill that empowers us as decision-makers and leaders too. So, tell me, how has your skating experience shaped your confidence, both on and off the wheels?"

Michael was the first to share his thoughts. "When I first started skating, I was hesitant and unsure of myself," he admitted. "But with practice and perseverance, I gradually built confidence in my ability to glide smoothly and tackle obstacles. Similarly, in my role as a leader, I've learned that confidence comes from experience and knowledge. By continuously honing my skills and learning from both successes and failures, I've become more confident in making decisions and guiding my team."

Alex nodded in agreement, adding his perspective. "Skating taught me the importance of believing in myself and trusting my instincts," he said. "As a leader, confidence is essential for inspiring and motivating my team. When I exude confidence in my decisions and actions, it creates a sense of trust and stability within the team, empowering them to perform at their best."

Sarah shared a similar sentiment, reflecting on her journey to confidence in both skating and leadership. "Skating pushed me out of my comfort zone and forced me to confront my fears," she explained. "Through perseverance and resilience, I developed the confidence to take risks and push myself beyond my limits. In my role as a leader, I've learned to embrace challenges with the same level of confidence, knowing that failure is just another opportunity to learn and grow."

Brian spoke up, offering his perspective as well. "Balance isn't just about staying upright - it's also about staying mentally focused under pressure," he stated. "Skating honed my ability to remain calm and collected, even when faced with unexpected wobbles or challenging maneuvers. As a leader, confidence translates to remaining composed and clear-headed in the face of uncertainty. When I maintain confidence in myself and my team's abilities, we can navigate challenges more effectively and work together to achieve success."

Charlotte listened attentively, nodding as each team member shared their insights. When everyone had spoken, she summarized the key takeaways. "It's clear that building confidence is a journey, not a destination," she remarked.

"It requires courage, perseverance, and a willingness to believe in ourselves. Whether gliding on wheels or leading a team, confidence thrives on embracing challenges, learning from experiences, and trusting our abilities to overcome obstacles."

With a purposeful edge in her voice, Charlotte challenged the team to translate these lessons into their work environment. "Let's carry the confidence we gained here today back into our daily routines," she urged. "Each of you has demonstrated incredible resilience and determination on the rink. I have no doubt you can channel that same energy into your roles within your organization. Remember, the stronger your self-belief, the more it shines through in your work, from communication to the results we deliver as a team."

"Today has been incredibly productive," she continued, her eyes scanning the faces of those gathered around. "We've explored some critical areas of team development, including communication, balance, and confidence—all through the lens of roller skating."

"As we adjourn for the evening, let's take a moment to acknowledge the progress we've made and the insights we've gained. Each of you has shown a commitment to growth and a willingness to embrace change, and I have no doubt that we'll carry this momentum into our final day tomorrow."

Setting the Stage for the Finale

Looking ahead to day three, Charlotte outlined the agenda, ensuring it aligned with Brian's objectives for the retreat. "Tomorrow, we'll focus on addressing productivity head-on," she announced.

The team dispersed, eager to recharge for the final leg of their retreat journey. As they retreated for the night, the promise of another day of growth and discovery filled the air, setting the stage for a transformative conclusion to their roller skating retreat.

CHAPTER 11

Minimizing Distractions

‿‿

With the final day of their retreat underway, Charlotte welcomed the team with a warm smile, feeling a sense of anticipation for the day ahead.

"Good morning, everyone," Charlotte began, her voice filled with excitement. "I hope you all had a restful evening and are feeling refreshed and ready to dive into our final day together."

Pausing for a moment to allow her words to resonate, Charlotte continued, "Over the past two days, we've explored a range of topics, from communication and teamwork to balance and confidence."

"Now, as we embark on our last day, it's time to harness the lessons we've learned and apply them to enhance productivity and teamwork," Charlotte announced, her tone brimming with determination. "But before we jump into our workshop sessions, let's kick things off with a fun icebreaker activity on the rink. It's a great way to energize the team and foster a sense of camaraderie."

Leading the team to the skating rink, Charlotte's excitement was contagious as she explained the icebreaker activity. "Today, we're going to play a game called 'Skate

Tag." Her announcement was met with eager murmurs of anticipation from the team.

The rules were simple: one person would be "it" and skate around trying to tag others, who would then join in the pursuit until everyone was caught.

Amidst laughter and excitement, the team dispersed onto the rink, weaving and dodging, thoroughly enjoying the playful competition and bonding experience.

After several rounds of exhilarating gameplay, Charlotte called everyone back together, their faces flushed with excitement and smiles stretching from ear to ear.

Minimizing Distractions Workshop

"Fantastic job, everyone!" Charlotte exclaimed, clapping her hands together. "That was a wonderful way to kick off our final day together. Now that we're warmed up and invigorated, let's head back to the conference room and dive into our productivity workshop."

As the team settled back into the conference room, Charlotte seamlessly transitioned to the workshop on minimizing distractions for enhanced productivity.

"Thank you all for your enthusiasm on the rink," Charlotte began. "Now, let's shift our focus to a topic crucial for maximizing our productivity: minimizing distractions."

She projected the title of the workshop onto the screen: "Minimizing Distractions for Enhanced Productivity."

"Distractions can be like obstacles on the rink," Charlotte began, drawing a parallel between their skating experiences and workplace challenges. "Just like dodging other skaters or resisting the temptation of delicious snacks from the snack bar, we encounter various distractions in our work environment that can derail our focus and productivity."

She continued, "So, what exactly are distractions? Distractions are anything that pulls our attention away from the task at hand, making it harder for us to concentrate and perform effectively. They come in many forms, but some common sources of distractions in the workplace include noise, interruptions, and digital devices."

Charlotte paused, allowing her words to sink in before proceeding. "Imagine trying to focus on a complex task while your coworker's phone keeps ringing loudly, or when you're constantly bombarded with emails and notifications on your computer," she explained. "These distractions can disrupt our flow and make it challenging to stay on track."

She then shared examples of how distractions can impact productivity and focus, eliciting nods of recognition from the team. "Think about a time when you were deeply engrossed in a project, only to be interrupted by a colleague asking a question or by the sudden ping of a new message on your phone," Charlotte prompted. "It can take several minutes to regain your focus after such interruptions, leading to wasted time and reduced productivity."

Identifying Personal Distractions

As the team members reflected on their own experiences with distractions, Charlotte could see them recognizing the significance of the issue and the need to address it proactively.

Charlotte led the team through a self-assessment exercise, prompting them to reflect on their typical workday and identify specific distractions they encountered. Many team members shared their experiences, recognizing patterns of distraction in their own routines.

"I often find myself getting sidetracked by emails and instant messages," Emily admitted, nodding in agreement as others chimed in with similar experiences. "It's like a constant battle to stay focused on my tasks."

James shared his struggle with noise distractions in the office. "With an open floor plan, it's hard to concentrate when there's so much background chatter," he explained. "I end up putting on headphones just to drown out the noise, but even then, it's not always effective."

Michael spoke up about the challenge of digital distractions. "I'm guilty of checking my phone too often, especially when I'm waiting for a response or feeling bored," he confessed. "It's like a reflex, but I know it's not helping me stay productive."

Charlotte acknowledged his honesty, nodding in agreement. "Digital distractions are a major culprit for many of us," she admitted. "The constant stream of emails, notifications, and social media updates can easily pull us away from focused work."

As each team member shared their experiences, Charlotte listened attentively, taking note of the common themes and challenges they faced. She could sense a shared frustration among the group, but also a determination to find solutions and improve their focus and productivity.

"Thank you all for sharing your experiences," Charlotte said, once the discussion had quieted down. "It's clear that distractions are a significant issue for many of us, but the good news is that there are strategies we can use to minimize their impact."

Attention Residue: The Mental Burden

The discussion examined the effects of distractions on productivity and well-being. Charlotte explained the concept of attention residue and how switching between tasks can diminish efficiency. The team listened attentively, realizing the magnitude of the problem.

"Attention residue is like carrying a mental burden from one task to another," Charlotte elaborated. "Even after we switch tasks, our minds remain partially engaged with the previous task, reducing our cognitive resources for the new task."

Understanding the impact of attention residue, the team began to grasp how seemingly innocuous distractions could significantly hinder their productivity. They nodded in agreement as Charlotte shared research findings highlighting the detrimental effects of multitasking and frequent interruptions on cognitive performance.

Strategies for Distraction Management

Charlotte then presented a range of strategies and techniques for managing distractions in the workplace. She emphasized methods such as time-blocking, creating a dedicated workspace, and practicing mindfulness. Real-life examples and success stories added credibility to the strategies.

"I've found that time-blocking helps me stay focused on specific tasks without getting pulled in different directions," Sarah shared, reflecting on her own experience. "By setting aside dedicated blocks of time for different types of work, I can minimize distractions and make better progress."

Michael nodded in agreement, adding, "Creating a dedicated workspace has been a game-changer for me. Having a designated area free from distractions helps me get into the right mindset for focused work."

Charlotte encouraged the team to experiment with different strategies and find what worked best for each of them. She stressed the importance of consistency and perseverance in implementing distraction management techniques, acknowledging that it might take time to see significant improvements.

Creating a Focus-Friendly Workspace

"As we continue to refine our approach to managing distractions, let's remember that it's a journey," Charlotte concluded, her tone hopeful yet pragmatic. "By being mindful of our environment, setting boundaries, and prioritizing focus, we can reclaim our time and energy for meaningful work."

"Your workspace should support your ability to concentrate and minimize distractions," Charlotte explained. "Let's explore some strategies for achieving that."

She encouraged the team to consider factors such as lighting, noise levels, and ergonomic setup when configuring their physical workspace. Charlotte also emphasized the importance of organizing digital tools and minimizing digital clutter to reduce cognitive load and increase efficiency.

"Think about how you can streamline your digital workspace to enhance your focus," Charlotte suggested. "This could involve decluttering your desktop, organizing files and folders, and using productivity tools to manage tasks and deadlines."

As the team members brainstormed ideas and shared insights, Charlotte circulated among them, offering guidance and encouragement. She highlighted the importance of creating a workspace that felt comfortable and conducive to deep work, tailored to each individual's preferences and needs.

Personalizing Your Workspace for Success

"Your workspace should be a reflection of your unique work style and preferences," Charlotte reminded them. "By optimizing your environment for focus and productivity, you can set yourself up for success in tackling your daily tasks and projects."

The workshop concluded with a brainstorming session where team members exchanged ideas and committed to implementing distraction management techniques in their daily routines.

As the team broke for lunch, Charlotte couldn't help but feel proud of the progress they had made and looked forward to the remainder of their final day together, confident that they would continue to grow and thrive as a cohesive and productive team.

CHAPTER 12

Prioritizing for Productivity

$$\approx$$

As the team reconvened after lunch, Charlotte greeted them with a smile, ready to delve into the next topic.

"Welcome back, everyone," Charlotte began. "I hope you enjoyed your break and are feeling refreshed."

With everyone settled, Charlotte posed a question to the group, "How do you typically decide what tasks to work on first at the start of your day?"

Several team members chimed in, sharing that they often begin by checking their emails to ensure they are responsive and up to date.

"Emails are important for communication, but they aren't necessarily the most productive use of our time," Charlotte explained, nodding in agreement with their responses. "Instead, I recommend prioritizing tasks based on the energy they require."

She elaborated, "If you have the most mental energy in the morning, start with the biggest tasks that require deep concentration. Conversely, if you need some time to wake up, begin with smaller, less mentally demanding tasks to ease into the day."

"But Charlotte," asked Emily. "What if our mornings are filled with back-to-back meetings or urgent requests from clients? How do we find the time to prioritize tasks based on energy levels?"

Charlotte nodded, acknowledging Emily's valid concern. "That's a common challenge, Emily," she replied. "While it's true that mornings can be hectic, it's important to carve out dedicated time for focused work whenever possible."

Sarah chimed in, voicing a similar concern. "I often feel pressure to respond to emails and messages as soon as they come in, even if they're not urgent," she admitted. "How can we resist the urge to check our inbox constantly and prioritize tasks more effectively?"

Charlotte nodded in understanding. "It's understandable to feel the pressure to be responsive, Sarah," she empathized. "But, constantly checking your inbox can be a significant source of distraction and disrupt your focus. Remind me to come back to this when we dive into scheduling."

Adapting to the Unexpected

James raised his hand, adding another layer to the discussion. "What about unexpected interruptions or urgent tasks that arise throughout the day?" he asked. "How do we adapt our prioritization strategy in those situations?"

Charlotte nodded appreciatively at James's question. "Flexibility is key, James," she replied. "While it's important to have a plan in place, it's equally important to remain adaptable and responsive to changing circumstances."

She advised, "When unexpected interruptions occur, take a moment to assess their urgency and impact on your current priorities. If necessary, adjust your task list accordingly and communicate with your team or manager about any changes to your workload."

The Power of Focus

Having addressed the team's concerns, Charlotte transitioned to discussing the detrimental effects of multitasking. She emphasized the importance of focusing on one task at a time and avoiding the temptation to juggle multiple tasks simultaneously.

"Task switching is a waste of mental energy and significantly reduces productivity," she explained. "It's best to have a list of priorities, no more than three, and focus solely on those tasks without distraction."

She continued, "If you have multiple important projects on your plate, seek clarification from your manager on which one should take precedence. Having a clear understanding of priorities helps minimize ambiguity and ensures that you're working on the most impactful tasks."

"And finally," Charlotte continued, "A good rule of thumb is to create a prioritized list of tasks for each project, breaking them down into manageable chunks. This will help you feel a sense of progress and momentum as you work towards your goals," she advised.

As Charlotte concluded her remarks, the team members nodded thoughtfully, taking notes and mentally planning how they would implement these strategies starting Monday when they returned to the office. They were eager to put their newfound knowledge into action and improve their productivity and focus.

To solidify their learning and prepare for the final session, Charlotte announced, "Let's take a quick 15-minute break to stretch our legs and recharge. We'll reconvene shortly for our final workshop on scheduling."

CHAPTER 13

Scheduling Strategies

~~~

As the team reconvened after their break, Charlotte distributed papers to everyone, each containing a list of five scheduling strategies. She explained the purpose of the exercise: to review each strategy together and ultimately commit to implementing one of them.

"We've discussed the importance of effective scheduling and time management," Charlotte began. "Now, let's explore these strategies together and identify which ones resonate most with each of us."

Addressing Sarah's concern from the prioritization workshop, Charlotte suggested, "Sarah, you mentioned feeling pressured to respond to emails and messages immediately. One strategy that can help with this is time blocking. Just allocate specific blocks of time for checking and responding to emails so you can resist the urge to constantly check your inbox and focus on other tasks. You can do the same for pretty much everything you have on your plate. By blocking time for specific activities in advance, you can have more clarity about when it's going to get done. But once you set that time on your calendar, you have to respect it."

"I know we kind of covered this with James' question earlier, but I've got to ask," began Sarah. "I can see the value in time blocking, Charlotte, and I appreciate the suggestion. But, I'm worried about how to adapt it to my workflow, especially when my tasks and priorities can change throughout the day. What if I allocate time for emails and then something urgent comes up that requires immediate attention? I'm concerned that sticking too rigidly to a schedule might make it difficult to respond effectively to unexpected demands."

"I completely understand your concern, Sarah. Flexibility is crucial, especially in a dynamic work environment where priorities can shift suddenly. While time blocking provides structure, it's important to remain adaptable. One way to address this challenge is to build in some buffer time within your schedule. This buffer time can serve as a cushion to accommodate unexpected tasks or emergencies that arise throughout the day."

"For example," Sarah continued, "You could allocate specific time blocks for your core tasks and then leave some open slots for handling unforeseen issues or responding to urgent emails. This way, you maintain a balance between structured time for focused work and the flexibility to address changing priorities as they arise."

"It may take some trial and error to find the right balance that works for you, Sarah," said Charlotte. "I recommend starting with a flexible approach to time blocking and refining it over time based on what works best for your workflow. Remember, the goal is to enhance productivity while still allowing room for adaptation and responsiveness to changing circumstances."

"I see what you're saying, Charlotte," Sarah responded, her expression reflective. "Building in buffer time sounds like a practical approach to handle unexpected tasks without feeling overwhelmed. I'll definitely give it a try and see how it works for me."

Charlotte smiled, pleased to see Sarah's willingness to try new approaches. "You're welcome, Sarah. Remember, productivity is all about finding what works best for you and adapting as needed."

"How do you determine how much buffer time to allocate between tasks?" James asked. "I worry about overestimating or underestimating the time needed and throwing off my entire schedule."

Charlotte responded, "That's a valid concern, James. It's important to strike a balance between allowing enough buffer time for unforeseen delays without allocating too much time and reducing productivity. One approach is to start with a conservative estimate and adjust based on your experience over time."

"The strategy that caught my attention is avoiding overcommitting," Michael said. "I often find myself saying yes to too many tasks and then feeling overwhelmed trying to complete them all."

Charlotte nodded in agreement. "Overcommitting can lead to burnout and decreased productivity," she affirmed. "It's essential to be mindful of our capacity and learn to say no to tasks or projects that don't align with our priorities."

Emily chimed in, "Personally, I like the idea of batching similar tasks together. It seems like it would help minimize context switching and increase efficiency."

"That's a great point, Emily," Charlotte replied. "Batching similar tasks allows us to streamline our workflow and maintain focus on similar types of work, which can improve productivity."

"I find the idea of breaking tasks into smaller steps particularly helpful," Alex remarked. "It can be overwhelming to tackle a big project all at once, but breaking it down into smaller, more manageable tasks makes it feel more achievable."

As the discussion continued, the team members shared their insights and perspectives on each strategy. They identified which ones resonated most with their own work styles and challenges.

After reviewing all the strategies, Charlotte concluded, "It's clear that each of these strategies offers valuable tools for improving our scheduling and time management skills. By committing to implementing just one of these strategies, we can take a significant step towards becoming more efficient and productive."

The team members took turns sharing which strategy they had chosen and why. Some opted for time blocking to better allocate their time, while others chose to prioritize tasks more effectively or avoid overcommitting.

"To be productive, we have to be intentional about how we structure our time and prioritize our tasks," Charlotte remarked. "By incorporating these strategies into our daily routines, we can optimize our productivity and achieve our goals more effectively."

The team concluded the scheduling workshop, ready to put their chosen strategies into practice starting Monday.

CHAPTER 14

Aligning Culture and Goals

~~~

After a short break, the team gathered for their next discussion. Charlotte began by engaging the team with a rhetorical question, "Remember when you were out there skating? Think back to how you were impacted by the music. Did you notice how certain songs moved you and others made you want to stop skating?"

As the team nodded in agreement, recalling their experiences on the rink, Charlotte explained. "In the same way that the music on the rink influenced your skating experience, your company culture influences your work environment, your experience at work, and ultimately, your productivity," Charlotte explained. "The atmosphere created by the music mirrors the vibe set by our culture. When the music resonates, you feel engaged and inspired. When it doesn't resonate, you become disengaged and your performance tanks."

"But that's not all. There are other similar parallels that I want you to think about as we bring our time together to a close." Charlotte went on to explain the significance of each element in the analogy. "The skaters represent us, the employees," she continued. "Our skills and resources, our 'skates,' determine how well we navigate the rink and achieve our goals. Now, let's say that the number of times you circle the rink is akin to your productivity at work. What this means is that it takes a skilled, motivated, and engaged employee to create results," Charlotte explained. "But like skaters who may stumble and fall, we also make mistakes along the way. We get distracted by the smells from the concession stand and the sounds from the arcade games, by the skaters who cross our paths, even by our own mind as we skate. What's important when you get off track is that you bring yourself back, you learn from your mistakes, and you grow from these experiences. They are a fertile breeding ground for creating new productivity strategies."

"Your company culture should not only reflect who you are but also where you want to go," Charlotte emphasized. "By aligning your culture with your organizational goals, you can create an environment that fosters productivity, creativity, and employee satisfaction."

She encouraged the team to reflect on their company's current culture and how it aligned with the organization's goals. "Are there aspects of the culture that support your goals? Are there areas where we need to make adjustments or improvements?" Charlotte prompted, inviting open discussion.

As the team shared their thoughts and insights, Charlotte facilitated the conversation, guiding them towards identifying areas for alignment and improvement.

Together, they brainstormed strategies for reinforcing positive aspects of the culture while addressing any discrepancies that might hinder progress towards their goals.

By the end of the discussion, the team had identified actionable steps for aligning their company culture with organizational goals.

CHAPTER 15

Skating Your Own Path

〜

As the team wrapped up their discussion on aligning culture and goals, Charlotte segued seamlessly into the next topic, "Skating Your Own Path." With a warm smile, she encouraged the team to reflect on their individuality and personal development.

"Each of you brings a unique set of skills, experiences, and perspectives to the table," Charlotte began, her voice infused with encouragement. "It's important to recognize and embrace these differences as they are what make your team strong and diverse."

She prompted the team to consider their strengths and weaknesses, emphasizing the value of self-awareness in personal and professional growth. "Take a moment to reflect on your strengths—those innate qualities and talents that set you apart," Charlotte suggested. "But don't forget to acknowledge your weaknesses as well. They are opportunities for growth and development."

Charlotte shared anecdotes from her own journey, highlighting moments of challenge and triumph. "I've found that embracing both my strengths and weaknesses has been instrumental in my own growth," she admitted.

"It's through facing challenges and overcoming obstacles that we truly discover our potential."

Encouraging the team to do the same, Charlotte urged them to embrace their individuality and strive for continuous improvement. "Skating your own path means honoring who you are while also pushing yourself to be the best version of yourself," she explained. "It's about celebrating your successes and learning from your failures."

Throughout the discussion, Charlotte fostered an environment of openness and acceptance, inviting team members to share their reflections and aspirations. "I encourage each of you to take some time to reflect on your journey so far," she said. "Consider what you've learned about yourself and how you can leverage your strengths to achieve your goals."

As the team engaged in introspection, Charlotte circulated among them, offering encouragement and support. She listened attentively to their stories, offering guidance and perspective where needed.

Brian opened up about the transformative journey the retreat had been for him. "Previously," he confessed with a touch of vulnerability, "I felt the weight of all responsibilities on my back. But through the discussions and insights we've gained, I've come to realize that it's okay to ask for help. I don't have to carry the weight of the world on my shoulders. We're a team, and we're here to support each other."

Sarah followed, reflecting on her tendency towards perfectionism and control. "I've always had high standards for myself and for others," she confessed, a hint of self-awareness in her tone. "But I've come to realize that holding onto this need for control was hindering both my own growth and the team's progress. By releasing some of that control and allowing others to take initiative, I've seen a remarkable improvement in our collaboration and productivity."

Emily spoke next, her voice resonating with a newfound sense of determination. "I've always been the type to put others' needs before my own, often at the expense of my own well-being," she shared. "But through this retreat, I've learned the importance of setting boundaries and prioritizing self-care. When I take better care of myself, I've found that I'm actually able to give more to others and contribute more effectively to the team."

Lastly, Lisa bravely shared her personal journey, acknowledging the challenges she faced due to her sensory disability. "It's no secret that my weaknesses are more evident than most," she began, her voice unwavering. "But I've come to realize that my strengths lie in my unique perspective and abilities. I have a knack for mapping information in my head, for coming up with creative solutions to problems, and because I'm vocal about my situation, I bring attention to special needs within the team. My disability doesn't define me—it's just one part of who I am."

A Symphony of Strengths

As the final reflections echoed through the room, a powerful silence descended. It wasn't the silence of awkwardness, but one of profound understanding. Each team member had peeled back layers of self-perception, revealing not just flaws and strengths, but a unique tapestry woven from experiences, skills, and perspectives.

The vulnerability they'd displayed wasn't weakness, but a testament to the trust they'd built. Now, they saw each other not as a collection of individual notes, but as the instruments in a magnificent orchestra. Each member possessed a distinct voice, yet together, they had the potential to create a symphony that transcended their individual limitations.

The nervous energy that had fueled their initial interactions had morphed into a shared determination. They understood that their success wasn't about erasing differences, but about learning to harmonize them. By leveraging their collective strengths, they could navigate any obstacle.

A smile slowly spread across Charlotte's face. This wasn't just the culmination of a workshop; it was the birth of a team in the truest sense of the word. Gone were the days of isolated individuals, tossed together by happenstance. This team had undergone a metamorphosis, transforming into a powerful unit.

As the session concluded, the team didn't walk out with a rigid plan, but with a feeling like anything was possible. They were ready to face the challenges ahead, not with trepidation, but with the exhilarating knowledge that they had the power to create something extraordinary, one well-placed note at a time.

CHAPTER 16

The Final Lap

≈

As the retreat drew to a close, the team gathered one last time on the roller rink, ready to reflect on their journey and celebrate their growth together.

Charlotte, her voice filled with pride, addressed the team, "Let's take a moment to celebrate the incredible journey we've shared on this rink. Each of you has grown in remarkable ways, both individually and as a team."

For their finale, Charlotte proposed a unique activity. "Let's form a human line, from Tim to me, stretching across the rink. One by one, you'll skate down the line, a champion gliding towards the finish line." Her smile widened. "But the real finish line is here, with your colleagues, ready to celebrate you."

A cheer erupted as the team members formed the line, their faces beaming with a newfound camaraderie. Lisa and Ashley, the first to go, navigated the human gauntlet with laughter and high fives. Reaching Charlotte, they received warm embraces and genuine congratulations. Then, they rejoined the back of the line, eager to witness the celebration of their teammates.

As each team member skated down the line, a wave of cheers and encouragement washed over them. There were pats on the back, knowing nods, and genuine smiles. It was a powerful display of the respect and trust they had built over the retreat.

Finally, it was Brian's turn. He skated towards Charlotte with a sense of determination, his gaze fixed on the finish line. As he reached her, he paused for a moment, taking in the significance of the moment.

"Thank you for believing in me," Brian said to Charlotte, his voice filled with emotion. "I've learned that I don't have to do it all on my own, and that's a lesson I'll carry with me forever."

With a final high-five, Brian joined the rest of the team at the end of the line.

And then, as the perfect ending to their retreat, the team broke out into a celebratory dance party on wheels, gliding and spinning to the beat of "Boogie Wonderland" by Earth, Wind & Fire. The rink was filled with laughter and joy as they let loose and celebrated their accomplishments together.

Supercharge Your Productivity

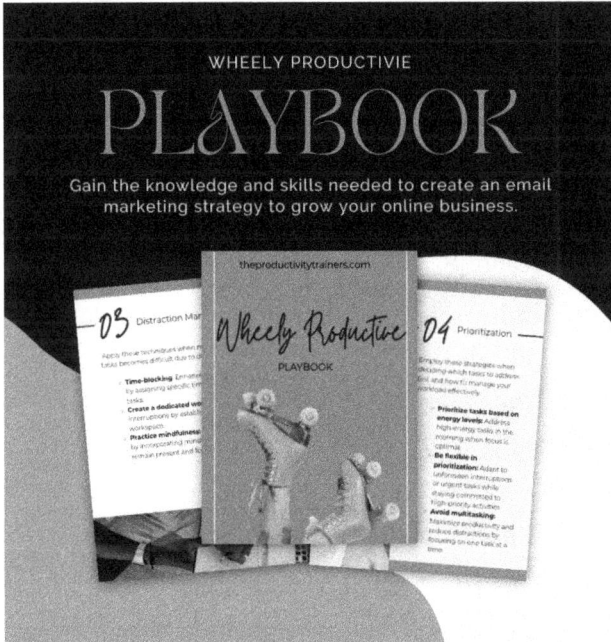

Want to take action on the game-changing strategies from this book?

Download your FREE copy of the "Wheely Productive Playbook" and unlock a treasure trove of practical tools and insights to boost your personal and team productivity.

Here's what you'll find inside:

- **Conquer Distractions:** Master distraction-busting techniques to stay focused and maximize your output.

- **Prioritize Like a Pro:** Learn the art of prioritizing tasks based on energy levels and changing priorities.

- **Time Management on Wheels:** Take control of your schedule with time-blocking, realistic deadlines, and efficient task organization.

- **Culture Meets Goals:** Discover how to create a culture that fuels individual and organizational success.

- **Embrace Your Uniqueness:** Identify your strengths and weaknesses to personalize your path to peak productivity.

- **The Final Victory Lap:** Celebrate your wins, cultivate team spirit, and empower each other for ongoing success.

Ready to roll into action? Download your FREE copy of the "Wheely Productive Playbook" today at: www.drsharongrossman.com/playbook

Empower Your Team

Inspired by Brian's success story? Dr. Sharon Grossman, the mastermind behind the roller rink retreat, offers a range of services to help small to medium-sized companies achieve similar breakthroughs. From team building and corporate training to consulting, executive coaching, and retreats, Dr. Grossman's expertise can empower your organization.

Get in touch at: www.drsharongrossman.com

Also by Sharon Grossman

The Solution to Burnout: 7 Steps from Exhausted to Extraordinary

How to Train Your Brain for Success in 5 Steps

The Stress Advantage: Lessons from the Tennis Court

Get them at: drsharongrossman.com/books

About the Author

Dr. Sharon Grossman is a powerhouse of productivity. With over 20 years of experience as a therapist and executive coach, she leverages her psychology background to empower individuals and teams. Dr. Grossman is not only the author of several books, but also a sought-after business consultant and keynote speaker.

Through her company, The Productivity Trainers, Dr. Grossman's mission is clear: to guide teams from overwhelmed to optimal performance, all without burning out.

When she's not helping teams reach their full potential, Sharon enjoys life in Miami Beach, Florida with her husband and two children.

Connect with Dr. Sharon:

- Website: www.DrSharonGrossman.com
- LinkedIn: @sharongrossman

www.ingramcontent.com/pod-product-compliance
Lightning Source LLC
Chambersburg PA
CBHW060413050426
42449CB00009B/1963